James,
Enjoy your Journey!
Katuna

3/30/06
James,
The path is the goal!
The journey is the reward.
R Sill

James—
Remember that discovering where you want to go is half the fun! Enjoy the ride.
Aloha

The Road to HAPPY

Discovering and Navigating Your Journey

Randall HENION
Katrina REDMON
C.J. JOSEPH

The Road to Happy

First edition 2004
Copyright © 2004 by Randall Henion, Katrina Redmon, and C.J. Joseph

All rights reserved. No part of the contents of this book may be reproduced or transmitted in any form or by any means, electronic or mechanical, including photocopying, recording, or by any information storage and retrieval system without prior written permission from the author.

ISBN 1-930154-13-5

Printed in Canada

10 9 8 7 6 5 4 3 2 1

Book design and production by Whitline Ink Incorporated
(336) 367-6914 ——————— www.whitlineink.com

Contents

• • •

Read this First...7
Happiness and Health....................................11
Instructions..13
The Scope of a Life......................................15
Personal Pieces..17

——————————————————————————Concept Phase

CHAPTER 1
Defining Your Dreams: Designing Your Life 25

CHAPTER 2
Playing It Forward: The Refining Process 33

CHAPTER 3
Roadblocks and Obstacles: Getting Perspective................. 39

CHAPTER 4
Your Strengths and Challenges 43

CHAPTER 5
Priorities Checklist: What's Important to You................... 47

——————————————— Design Phase

CHAPTER 6
Designing Your Dream (and Your Life) 53
    Walk-Through List for Your Current House 55
    Walk-Through List for Your Dream House 58
    Assessing the Costs of Change 66

CHAPTER 7
Safety Training 69
    First-Aid Kit 69
    The Safety Rules 70

——————————————— Hard Hat Zone

CHAPTER 8
Clearing the Clutter 77

CHAPTER 9
Finalize the Design: Taking Inventory and Stocking Your Toolbox . 81
    Finalize Your Blueprint 82
    Stock Your Toolbox 83

CHAPTER 10
Developing Your Construction Schedule 89

——————————————— Completion

CHAPTER 11
Celebrate! 97

Epilogue: Life Is an Ever-Changing Journey 99
Bookshelf 101
Acknowledgements 103

Read this First

DEEP INSIDE EACH of us is the home where our soul lives. Throughout this book we use both the metaphor of a "home" as well as use your physical "house" (the place you live) to explore and describe yourself and how you exist in the world. Dream interpreters have referenced the "house" in a dream as a representation of yourself or aspects of your ego; we will be using it as a conscious way of looking at your life. In its rooms, attic, basement, and closets live our dreams, desires, memories, accomplishments, fears, and disappointments—all the aspects of who we have been, who we are, and who we want to be. It houses our past, present, and future.

This private inner home is reflected in how we physically present ourselves in the world. Is that too intellectual? Simply put, an unhappy person is the reflection of an unhappy soul. A happy person is the reflection of a happy soul.

Throughout history, people have named their homes. We have named this private inner home where our souls live "Happy." We asked our favorite street philosopher one day, "What is the most important thing in life?" Joshua responded, "Oh that's easy—to be happy." When reflecting on his comment, we realized it is easily stated, but difficult to achieve.

As with any home, without attention your soul will deteriorate. Without proper attention and care, we will feel that something is not right in our lives. We may know what the issues are; we may not and need to search for them. This deterioration can be in the form of general uneasiness, dissatisfaction, or loss of passion. Or it may be a feeling that something is missing—for instance, you feel tired or drained of energy or don't look forward to your work or personal activities.

When these feelings arise, it's time to walk through our inner home and determine what is behind the closed doors, stuffed in closets, or hidden under the beds that keeps us from living our lives to the fullest. We must face our issues and develop a plan to move forward. What's going on in our lives is a reflection of the junk (and treasures) we're storing on the inside.

It is often easier and safer to attempt to ignore the fact that something is calling out for our attention than it is to walk through the rooms of our lives and face our issues. However, for many of us a major event occurs that causes us to take another look at ourselves and to reassess what is important to us. This is when we begin exploring our home and making changes. It can be hard. It can be scary. It is definitely exciting.

As we go through this book, what we're really doing is "cleaning house." Then taking an inventory, and instead of a slapdash approach to decorating, we become an interior decorator, planning and making sure that everything "fits." Unlike some home improvement shows, we're making the decisions *and* doing the work. And when we've built a house we love, we're having a party!

We have many ways to make our home what we want it to be. We can renovate, remodel, or we can redesign and rebuild.

During this process, we must remember four things:

1) This is your life. Be who *you* want to be, not who someone else wants you to be; keep in mind what is important to *you*.
2) Your life is not a dress rehearsal; it's a live show filled with cameos and improvisations.
3) There is only one building code you must follow: Do no harm. The remainder of the rules are for you to determine.
    What the heck does "do no harm" mean? Remember that this is about you, the only thing you truly can control. It's not about blame, bending others to your will, or judging people and things for being different from what you would have them to be. Therefore, when you make changes you

need to come from a place of compassion, not revenge, punishment, or guilt. Some situations you will create may cause negative feelings in those around you; if you're acting with regard for yourself and respect for others instead of malice for them, their reaction is of their creation, rather than a result of your actions.

4) Your soul's home is private; you can invite those with whom you wish to share a piece of yourself and for whatever time period you choose. Like above in (3), do not allow others to harm you. Others can only harm you to the extent you allow them.

Happiness and Health

WHAT IS THE best reason for learning to be happy? It's good for you! Like vegetables without the green taste. More like dark chocolate—an endorphin rush that is an acquired taste.

According to the "Teach Health" Web site, being overstressed can tax many of our body's functions and result in fatigue and mystery aches, thyroid malfunction, irritable bowel syndrome, and of course, high blood pressure and heart problems. A recent finding stated that "bad fat is sad fat," citing that "People with clinical depression are about four times more likely to have a heart attack than other individuals."*

Mind, body, and spirit teacher Louise Hay talks about all disease coming from a state of unforgiveness—not just of others but of ourselves as well. One of my favorite thoughts from her book *You Can Heal Your Life* is: "Would you dig into yesterday's garbage to make tonight's meal? Do you dig into old mental garbage to create tomorrow's experiences?"

Keeping yourself in a guarded state or under a constant state of scrutiny (often to an unrealistic standard) expends a tremendous amount of energy, sometimes called stress. Most people have heard of the negative impacts of stress on heart rate, blood pressure, cholesterol levels, mental health, and a variety of other health issues. Being "true" to yourself allows you to focus your energy in areas that serve the needs of your body as well as your soul.

In *Choosing Happiness—The Art of Living Unconditionally*, author Veronica Ray dedicates an entire chapter to health and aging and the positive influence of happiness.

*Winston-Salem Journal Accent section, June 10, 2003

Intuitive health facilitator Lloyd Rawson echoes the concept that our bodies are a reflection of the mental and spiritual energy we carry with us—negative energy will eventually manifest itself physically; positive energy will manifest in robust health. But he also points out that holding onto negative energy and its mental patterns is a choice we can change.

Bottom line? Happiness is healthy.

D O N O T T U R N T H I S P A G E !

Instructions

THIS IS A WORKBOOK. "Work" implies there are activities and exercises to be done at a specific time and in a specific order. "Book"—although it is written words—implies an interactive guide.

This story (*your* story) unfolds as you personalize the exercises in each chapter, which will help you define and refine who you are or who you want to be.

Happiness does not drop into your lap. It is a deliberate effort on your part to focus your energy and efforts on what you value. It is setting healthy boundaries for those things that would pull you off the road. Your journey will be filled with bumps and curves and sometimes dead ends. This is part of being human. But your ability to get past them, smiling inside and out, is where happiness lives.

DISCLAIMER

BEFORE WE BEGIN anything, let us be perfectly clear about the fact that we, the authors, have made the assumption that you, our readers, are smart. If you feel that we have made a serious error in this judgment, please give this book to a friend and forget you ever saw it. No one, including us, can make decisions for you, unless you have signed that right over to them and they have consented to assume that responsibility—we have not. Buying a book and taking the steps in no way absolves you from personal responsibility for your actions or decisions, and we urge you always to consider carefully the associated cost of anything you do.

This book was written as a guide to making decisions about creating the life that you want and making a conscious decision to be happy.

We in no way guarantee that you will be happy. Nor do we guarantee you will always make the decision that will get you where you want to go in the most direct way. And we do not expect what you value and what makes you happy today will necessarily be the same thing that makes you happy ten years from now.

All this being said, have fun. This book is about many things: getting the life you want, being happy, alleviating stress in your life, finding balance, and, if nothing else, a fun road of self-discovery.

Bon voyage,
—*C.J., Katrina, and Randall*

The Scope of a Life

"That which you have not achieved, can hardly be called your own."
—*unknown author*

In trying to examine our lives for what made us how we are, we discovered that we can go back over our lives with a fine-tooth comb and attribute to a variety of calamitous events the traumas that caused us to stray from the road to being happy.

Then we asked, "Why are we spending so much time ruminating on what has already happened?" We can't change the past.

Our reality is now. We are here. We are aware of things that we would like to change. We are aware of past events pivotal to this awareness, and *that's* what should matter. We don't always have the luxury of choosing circumstances, but we always have the luxury of choosing our response to them.

Throughout the scope of a life—an unhappy or glorious childhood; trauma-filled, angst-ridden, or fabulous adolescence; successful or miserable marriages; accomplished or failed careers—there are events which alter how we perceive and respond to the events in our lives. Some of us have remarkable coping skills; others of us have none. Some people find strength in their intellect, some in their spirituality, and some in their emotional support systems. Some people have yet to find theirs.

On the following pages, each of us has taken a short, life-altering period in his or her life and discussed the process of moving through it on the "Road to Happy." We learned that the journey, not the end, is the key.

Personal Pieces

IN THE FOUR MONTHS preceding the date I was asked to write this piece, my life has been an exercise in coping. My father, the one person for whom I was always "enough," had a devastating stroke. While he was in recovery, my grandfather was found to have a gangrenous condition that required amputation of his toe. My marriage of fifteen years disintegrated. My forty-one-year-old brother was getting married for the first time. And to top it all off, my business was atrophying due to neglect.

So, I redid the legal and financial documents for my mom and grandparents. I arranged to be the point person for my grandfather with the nursing home and handled the re-checks with the surgeon (which are still on-going). I moved from my marital home into my parents' basement with only the things that meant a lot to me, which weren't many.

The catastrophes and related incidents are too numerous to mention—a B-movie director would have deemed my life during this period not credible enough for a bad script; that much crap couldn't happen to one person in such a short span of time.

Not far into this series of events I realized that the director would've been right. I found myself laughing at each new incident; it was so bad it was funny. What happened? Here's the shortcut route to the end results:

- Dad's home and recovering, and his finances turned out better than anticipated.
- Grandpa had one helluva attitude:

    Me: "Grandpa, do you understand what they're going to do?"
    Grandpa: "Yeah, they're going to take the toe."

Me: "Are you going to be OK with that?"
Grandpa: "Oh, yeah. Better they take it before it goes up my leg and they have to cut something important off. They're not getting near my p#@*! with a knife."

- My family was happy to have me move in with them (safe and not so stressed).
- My soon-to-be ex-husband took the news better than expected, although he still doesn't get what happened—or why. I'm sad that he seemed so blindsided…but it's September, and he's been gone since February (with the exception of a bad week in between), so the change in status is not that big an issue for me.
- My brother is now a married, home-owning, stepfather of two. This all happened within weeks of his marriage, due to a series of events that would demand their own made-for-TV movie.
- As for me, my health has improved, I have a place to live, and my business is taking a new turn—and I feel good about it. I haven't lost my sense of humor, the family is adjusting to all the changes, and happiness for me was just getting through the angst of making the decisions to change things. The changes themselves were a piece of cake, and this is a good place to be.

What does this all mean to me?

I've learned that the state of happiness is a passive condition (as evidenced by those who seek to attain it through chemical support and other artificial means). *It is not real.* The sense of accomplishment that goes with overcoming the obstacles life sets before us provides true happiness; and it is in that moment, where our ambition carries through these obstacles, that happiness is found. The attempt to move forward is not always successful and, therefore, happy. But a lack of ambition (seeking, growing) and an acceptance of, or resignation to, an undesirable situation, is surely a recipe for misery. It's in the journey, not the destination, where real happiness is found.

—C.J.

 1999—WHAT A MILESTONE year it was for me!

« Turned forty in April.
« In July, left a position I dearly loved and had worked seventeen years to attain.
« Almost died from a massive blood clot and stroke in October.
« Lost my father (suddenly) in December.

When I turned forty, I began to look at what I had accomplished in my life and the things I wanted to do that I had not found time to do yet.

When I left my job, I realized that I had the exciting, challenging, and rewarding career I wanted. Next, I wanted to make a few changes in order to enhance the other aspects of my life; sometimes I had paid too high a price for the success in this one area of my life.

Coming within hours of death was the push I needed to stop *planning* to live and to *begin living*. I had made the things I wanted to do wait until I did all the things I should do. It seemed there were always things I should do, and there was never time for the things I wanted and enjoyed. I knew this had to change. *I was going to change!*

When Daddy died in December, I realized that being true to myself and my happiness was a necessity, not a luxury that I could live without. I reevaluated all of my priorities and goals and shared these with individuals that would (and still do) support me.

Here are a few changes I made:

« I have given myself the freedom to have fun and laugh every day. I have been asked if a person can be as happy as I always seem to be. My answer? *Absolutely!*
« I take the time to bring joy, laughter, and a smile to others every day, hopefully enhancing their lives as much as doing this enhances mine.
« I enjoy today while making plans for tomorrow. I mix the "want to do's" and the "should do's." I take time for myself—physically, emotionally, mentally, socially, and financially.
« I no longer stay in relationships/situations that are not good

for me. I surround myself with relationships/situations in which I am passionate and that give me the challenges I need and enjoy.
- I live my own life, not the life others want me to live.
- I remind myself that I have friends who really love and care about me. (I never realized I had such devoted, loving friends until that scary October).
- I am basing my life on the knowledge that "nothing is impossible."

I have found peace, excitement, and love. I am growing every day and enjoying the process.

Life—bring it on. I'm ready!

—*Katrina*

 REFLECTING BACK ON my past fifty plus years, I realize that the good always outshines the bad. Going to ten different schools before graduating from high school made change a fact of life for me. Friends were not permanent, but the U-Haul trailer and moving were regular happenings. Until graduating from high school, I never lived anywhere more than three years. The change of location always gave way to a new and fresh start but left little room for long and lasting relationships.

School was no fun. My first day of class the teacher asked, "Randy Henion, what is wrong with you? Why do you keep moving so much?"

"I guess I have ants in my pants," I responded. The teacher didn't find it funny and pulled me to the front of the class and used a ping pong paddle to show me who was the boss.

I never did like school, sitting in rows and doing mundane tasks hour after hour. But after twelve years of school, I managed to graduate. I entered the Air Force on my eighteenth birthday. It was exactly what I needed to get my life in line and realize that I wanted to be more than a pawn for someone to spew orders upon.

My father, a good man at heart, was stricken with bleeding ulcers most of my childhood. As brilliant as he was, he allowed things to affect him so much that he never seemed to be happy much of the time. I can recall on fishing trips he would spew blood due to his nausea and upset stomach. It made me sad to see him so unhappy all the time. In spite of his ideas on education (the belief that a belt on his knee motivated me to learn spelling) I can remember mostly a family that was close and loving growing up. That foundation was a good building block.

After service and college, I found joy in working with adults to complete their education. It was sad to see how adults with so much potential were misdirected and misled because they didn't fit the mold. It encouraged me to help people find a new start and build upon the positives in their lives; they began to realize the future is ahead of them and not in the rear-view mirror of the past. After completion of graduate school and moving into senior administration of public schools, I realized that to make a difference one had to step out of the pack and be willing to take some heat and pressure.

My experience with a life of change made the public school system seem like a dynasty with a lot of little kings and queens. Even though lip service was given to letting all children have a chance, only a few were getting the cream of the educational experience. For the past twenty years or so, I have been dedicated to making a pathway for all kids to have good teachers and opportunities.

That path was not easy. Removing teachers who were not performing and administrators who were not doing their jobs was a difficult task, but it was a joy professionally to help make positive changes in the public schools.

Unfortunately, the joy of work took me away from the joy of living. I used to wish away vacations and weekends because I was excited to get on with the job. I think the fact that I was addicted to work that seemed to be a good cause left me with a void.

Now, at age fifty-six, my main objective is to make a positive difference. I realize that to do anything positive and to sustain energy, it's crucial to be happy personally. I am on the journey now, clearing the clutter and finding my way. It has been an exciting time getting to this point. And it seems the housework and restoration project before me is going to be a real joy.

The one thing I understand now more than ever is this: The future is what you see through the windshield and not the rear-view mirror. I am excited to share and experience the journey with new friends, and a few old ones, who seem to be in the same boat.

—Randall

Concept Phase

The concept phase is defining where to start:
- « Who you are.   *Who you want to be.*
- « What you have.   *What you would like to have.*
- « What is working for you.   *What is not working.*

Chapter 1

• • •

Defining Your Dreams: Designing Your Life

IMAGINE YOUR ideal self in the most beautiful place on earth. Carefully consider each of the following questions as you define and summarize your dream life in the following exercise:

- « What do you see around you?
- « How do you look?
- « How do you feel?
- « Where do you live? (Yes, you can have a brick traditional house on the sandy beach—no problem).
- « Custom design a set of friends and invite them into your house. Describe them.
- « Now imagine the perfect partner and invite that person inside. Describe him or her.
- « It's Monday morning. You're excited about your job and about going to work. Where do you go?
- « How are you dressed for this ideal job?
- « What do you do at this job?

CHAPTER ONE

« It's Friday evening and you have the weekend before you. What do you do for fun?

Now describe your <u>dream life</u> in detail:

I wake up refreshed I do maybe a 10-15 minute workout after freshening up 30 min workout every other day eat breakfast (light to moderate). I shower with wonderful shower oils and dress with the proper clothes for the season with all fitting well (comfortable). I am happy where I live now because bills are no concern I have lawn and garden people and a house keeper who I feel very good about. I have 2 cars a luxury car and a sports car both are payed for and will be there for a while. Maybe even a suv or F150. My wife has her own cars that she is totally responsible for. I go to work and my staff is already there at church I have in one office my Min. of Music and Production Asst. and on the other side my Sec, Treas. and personal asst. I am either dressed in shirt & tie with jacket in the car or suit. I didn't mention my motorcycle that I may ride, I have 2 of those. My salary from the 2 churches I pastor is $250,000 because I get $125,000 each. I receive $10,416.66 a month from each church and they both have about 500 members strong.

CHAPTER ONE

So this is your life, *right?* If not, why? Consider the current reality of your life and use the following questions to help you analyze where you are at this point. Think about the place in which you now live:

- « What do you see around you?
- « How do you look?
- « How do you feel?
- « Add in your current house.
- « Consider your current set of friends and invite them into your house. Describe them.
- « Think about your current partner and invite that person inside. Describe him or her.
- « It's Monday morning and you are about to go to work. Where do you go?
- « How are you dressed for your current job?
- « What do you do at your current job?
- « It's Friday evening and you have the weekend before you. What do you normally do for fun?

Now describe the <u>current reality</u> of your life in detail:

I have a very beautiful house around me, decorated and furnished. Today I am in sweats but it's a comfort thing today. I feel unclear about what I'm to do because there are several things pulling for my attention. I know I am in and out of stressful situations

My house is cool but the cash flow is not and I realize that we have created that situations for ourselves. I don't really have a "set" of friends just family I kind of do the same people or person all the time. My partner is just that because we partner in everything until it goes bad then its me alone. The partnership is one is the good for ideas and their is good for making it happen and Sometimes I feel that I'm being tired voraciously though. I go most of the time to change off to work, and I dress casual (nice). Most of the time I am bouncing between things without a sense of focus or project. For fun on Friday its maybe a movie.

CHAPTER ONE

Now that your dream life has been defined and you have reviewed your current reality, compare the two by looking at the similarities and differences.

List the similarities:

Your Dream Life	Your Current Reality
Nice home	Nice home
Great family	Great family
Motorcycle	Motorcycle

List the differences:

Your Dream Life	Your Current Reality
Finances flow free	Finances Don't flow free
Wife is self motivated	Wife lives through me
500 members (faithful)	50 faithful members

No differences? Close your book; you're finished. Accept our hearty congratulations. Pass this book to a friend.

If your book is still open...*welcome to the crossroads!*

YOU ARE HERE!

Your future starts here and now.

CHAPTER 2
• • •
Playing It Forward: The Refining Process

THESE ARE THE major questions in playing it forward:

« What will happen if you get what you asked for?
« What will happen if you don't?

If you stay on the road that brought you to where you are today...

« Where will you be in 10 years?

I will have gained a doctorate and still floundering not focused.

« What do you look like?

I am possibly 300+ pounds stressed or gray in a casket (dead).

CHAPTER TWO

« How do you feel?

After the last statement I feel sick (emotionaly).

« Where do you live?

In my own home. (nice home)

« Who are you with?

My wife daughter and foster daughter.

« When Monday comes, where will you go?

Maybe to Life construction or church

« How do you spend your weekends?

Preparing for Sunday and kind of following my wife

« Is this really what you want?

No

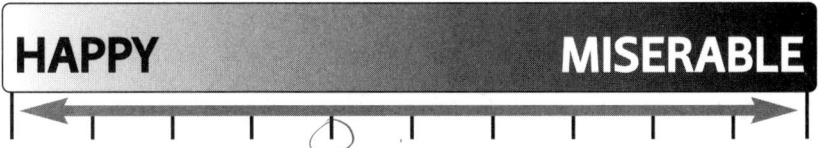

On a scale from happy to miserable, where are you?

_____

Now, let's take the other road: *your dream*. Remember, you have control of the outcome; it's your dream. Don't tell us that you don't know what would happen. Yes, you do! You have the control.

If you choose your dream:

« Where will you be in 10 years?

I will be traveling and see new things. In my very passionate state

« What do you look like?

Between 180-200 pounds, well groomed. I look like my message

« How do you feel?

Healthy fulfilled passionate focused.

CHAPTER TWO

« Where do you live?

Possibly in a very nice town house.

« Who will you be with?

My wife as she comes in from her office.

« When Monday comes, where will you go?

To my office complex and then to teach my 1 or 2 classes

« How do you spend your weekends?

Saturdays are on the lake or visiting a nice restaurant.

« Is this really what you want?

Yes

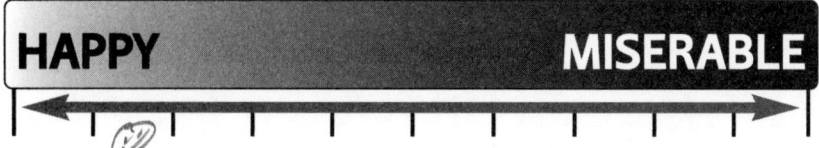

On a scale from happy to miserable, where would you be?

Playing It Forward: The Refining Process

« Have you made a choice? Yes or no?

Which will it be: the road of your current reality projected into the future or the road you custom designed for yourself?
« Which road do you choose to take? Why?

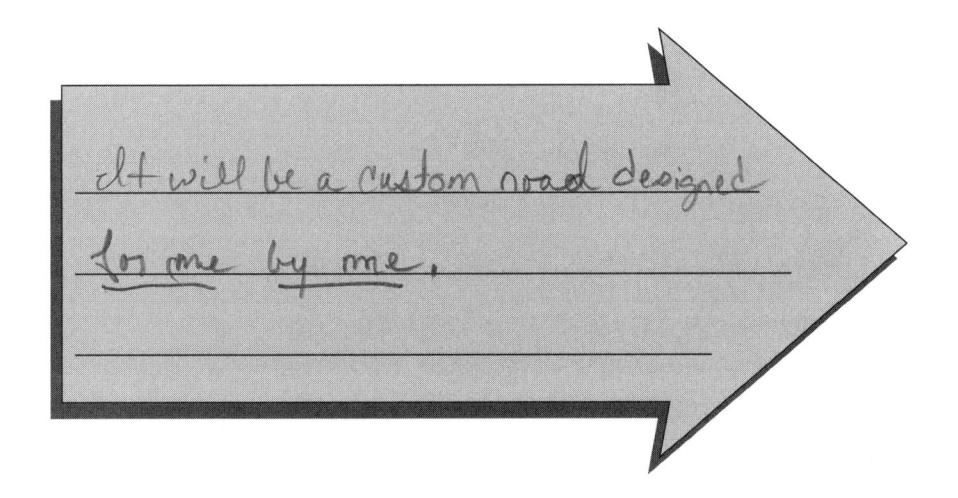

It will be a custom road designed for me by me.

CHAPTER 3

• • •

Roadblocks and Obstacles: Getting Perspective

NOW IT'S TIME for *excuses*. Excuses, excuses, excuses...yeah, yeah, yeah. But in your case, you may have a reason instead of an excuse. Let's get past the reasons, too.

─────────────── EXERCISE ───────────────

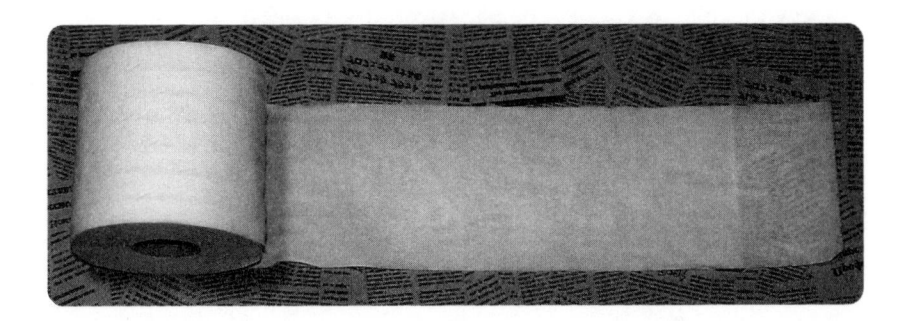

Go to the lavatory and get a roll of toilet paper. Think of all the reasons that you haven't made changes in your life. Write each of your reasons on a square of toilet paper, one reason per square. Tear into individual squares and set aside.

We'll help you get started with your potential reasons:

I haven't made changes because…

- « My problem is different.
- « I tried that once before.
- « I don't have the time/help/education/money…
- « It's impractical.
- « It looks good on paper, but…
- « My spouse/family/children/significant other won't approve.
- « It's too complicated.
- « It's too simple.

Let's see how you can get past these reasons. Don't think you *can* get past the reasons? Tripping on the path? When you fell learning to walk, didn't you just get up and go again? If a toddler can do it, you most definitely can do it!

It's time to analyze the squares of toilet paper:

« *My problem is different.*

Problems are as unique as we are individuals. The choice to make it a handicap is yours.
Example: Your parents are from another planet. (If this applies to anyone, please forward the paperwork to us. We'll buy them!)

« *I tried that once before.*

You learned to walk and talk. The expectation was that you *would* walk and talk. Did you do it the first time? No. Did you eventually? Yes. Why? You didn't give up. (You were too young to know about giving up.)

« *I don't have the time/help/education/money…*

Time: Everyone has the same number of hours in a day.
Help: You bought this book.

Education: Remember that education and knowledge are two different things.

Money: Is it money (or things money can buy) that you want?

« *It's impractical.*

Why is it impractical? How do you define impractical? Is happiness impractical? Please refer to the "Read this First" and "Happiness and Health" sections at the beginning of this book.

« *It looks good on paper, but...*

A written plan is just a tool. And *beware of but's*—extract your head and take a deep breath.

« *My spouse/family/children/significant other won't approve.*

It's *your* life. When you die, they won't go with you, so why should you live the life they prescribe for you? Do they not celebrate and share your successes? If they really love you, they will support you, as you support them. Remember, they have fears too.

« *It's too complicated.*

So you'd rather stay miserable? You can walk and breathe at the same time, right?

« *It's too simple.*

McDonald's was built on simplicity. Think of Post-Its (How hard are those to use?). The KISS method works in most cases (KISS: Keep It Simple, Stupid).

What are you afraid of? What are your excuses? If we missed your reason/excuse, let us know.

Time to flush the bullshit! Get up, go to the lavatory, and rid yourself of the roadblocks and obstacles by flushing all of these squares down the toilet.

> As a traveler on this path, you MUST wash your hands with soap and water to rid yourself of any residue and doubt before returning to this book.
>
> —*By order of the authors*

CHAPTER 4

• • •

Your Strengths and Challenges

YOU ARE THE ONLY constant in your plan. The strength to make the changes will come from within you. It's there; we're sure of it.

Take an inventory of your strengths. Make a list of all the nice things people have ever said about you (even if you didn't believe them).

<u>MY STRENGTHS</u>

I'm nice, I'm a awsome musician, I make things easy to understand. I'm humble, I'm a good communicator, I'm a good example and leader, I'm a blessing

CHAPTER FOUR

Your strengths are your tools. See the strengths in yourself as others have. Believe in these strengths and use them.

Although it's often hard to acknowledge your strengths, it's usually easy for you to think about your "weaknesses." Sometimes your "weaknesses" can get you into trouble, but we challenge you to review these perceived weaknesses and determine when and where these have served you well.

We'll get you started…

Perceived Weakness	How It Served You
« Have a temper.	Kept you from paying too much for a car repair.
« Too nice.	Received a note of thanks from someone, which brightened your day when you needed it most.
« Disorganized.	Allowed you time to spend with someone.
« Pushy.	Helped you negotiate a better deal.
« Not a good communicator.	Enabled you to be a good listener.
« Not a good listener.	Enabled you to take action.
Too nice	*People are always trying to enlist me*

Your Strengths and Challenges

Too busy	Have done a lot
Book worm/nerd	BA Religion, Minor Music, Masters Ad m.
Impulsive	Done a lot / Have a lot

Are these purely weaknesses? No. Each of these has a time and place to be a strength. Look how powerful you are! Look at all you have to draw upon. Look at *all* of your tools and realize how to utilize your perceived weaknesses to equip you better.

CHAPTER 5

• • •

Priorities Checklist: What's Important to You?

── Exercise ──

BEGIN BY FILLING in Column 1 within the chart on the following two pages with all the things that <u>are important to you.</u> Decide between the two indicated items the one that is more important. Only this priority will be carried forward to the next level (Column 2). Continue until you have narrowed the list down to "number one" in the last column—the absolute most important thing in your life.

CHAPTER FIVE

Column 1	Column 2	Column 3
Faith		
Wife 1.	Faith	
Family		Faith
Music	Family	
Education		
Church	Education	
Traveling		Education
Transportation	Transportation	
Home		
Friends	Friends	
Teaching		Friends
Movies	Teaching	
Exercise		
Dog	Exercise	
Dining out		Dinning out
Reading	Dinning out	

Priorities Checklist: What's Important to You?

PRIORITY CHART

Column 4   Column 5

Faith

Ta da! Your number one priority...

Faith

Friends

    Do you always give the item in your "number one" slot top priority? Do you give it much attention at all? Do you take it for granted? Have you decided to settle and do without it? Did you give up on it because it was too hard, you were too tired, or you settled for what you know rather than risk the unknown?

    As we move forward in Chapter 6, have the above in mind to keep perspective.

Design Phase

Deep inside each of us is the home where our souls live. In its rooms, attic, basement, and closets live our dreams, desires, memories, accomplishments, fears, and disappointments—all the aspects of who we have been, who we are, and who we want to be. It houses our past, present, and future.

Chapter 6

• • •

Designing Your Dream (and Your Life)

As you move to the next chapter, think about your attitude. Think of your view of the world, your life, and your dreams as your attitude. Do you often view the glass as half empty? Do you say things like, "I'll be happy when…" or "I'd be happy if…"? Or do you use a personal favorite such as, "Life is so hard!"?

A large part of happiness is spiritual and attitude based. Two people can look at the same picture and one will see beauty and the other only ugliness. Oftentimes it is our perception that creates our reality: If you can't see and appreciate the wonder of what goes on around you and your part in it, odds are that no amount of change is going to adjust your attitude enough to make you happy. You need to decide if you are going to be a victim of life or an active participant. If you can look at your dream objectively, you may realize that you are living it—you just haven't been seeing it clearly.

Arguably the most important item on the following Walk-Through List is "Windows." Just as your eyes are the windows to your soul, the windows in your house are a way of seeing your inner self. Windows give you a perspective both from the outside looking in, and from the inside looking out. Are they clear and bright? Are they dingy and make everything look old and dusty? Do you keep them open or shut? Do you have to have window treatments to hide behind, to re-frame everything? Or do you keep them open and free to see in and out and accept and appreciate life for what it is?

If you find that your perception and views are colored, covered, impaired, peppered with "if only…", "when…", and other qualifications, consider finding a resource to help you change your attitude before you decide what changes you need to make. If you think you're only slightly obscured, see numbered item 7 entitled "Clearing the view" in Chapter 7. Without a happy outlook, no amount of changes will create a dream that will bring you joy.

As you begin this design phase, remember that your happiness is the major factor in deciding where and when you want to spend your resources of time, energy, and money…happiness is a choice. It has been proven that happiness enables you to live longer, be healthier, and reduces stress. Therefore, happiness is not a luxury; happiness is a necessity.

Determining what makes you happy (by reviewing your priorities from the last chapter) will help you to decide whether to renovate, remodel, or bulldoze and rebuild.

Using the "Walk-Through List" you will complete on the following two pages, describe your current physical house or apartment in detail (not the minutiae, but do include color schemes, neatness factors, ambience, and other meaningful details). This physical house resembles how we physically present ourselves in the world at this time. Where you live now is a reflection of who you are—what you've created to this point in your life.

Walk-Through List for Your <u>Current</u> House

Location	Decription
« *Windows*	_____
	_____
« *Porch/front yard*	_____
	_____
« *Foyer*	_____
	_____
« *Kitchen*	_____
	_____
« *Dining room*	_____
	_____
« *Bedrooms*	_____
	_____
« *Living room*	_____
	_____
« *Laundry room*	_____
	_____

« *Family room* _____

_____

« *Study/library* _____

_____

« *Bathroom* _____

_____

« *Storage/closets/* _____
  basement

_____

« *Doors* _____

_____

« *Garage* _____

_____

« *Décor/artifacts* _____

_____

« *Bonus room or* _____
  anything omitted

_____

_____

Within the following grid, draw a blueprint of your current house:

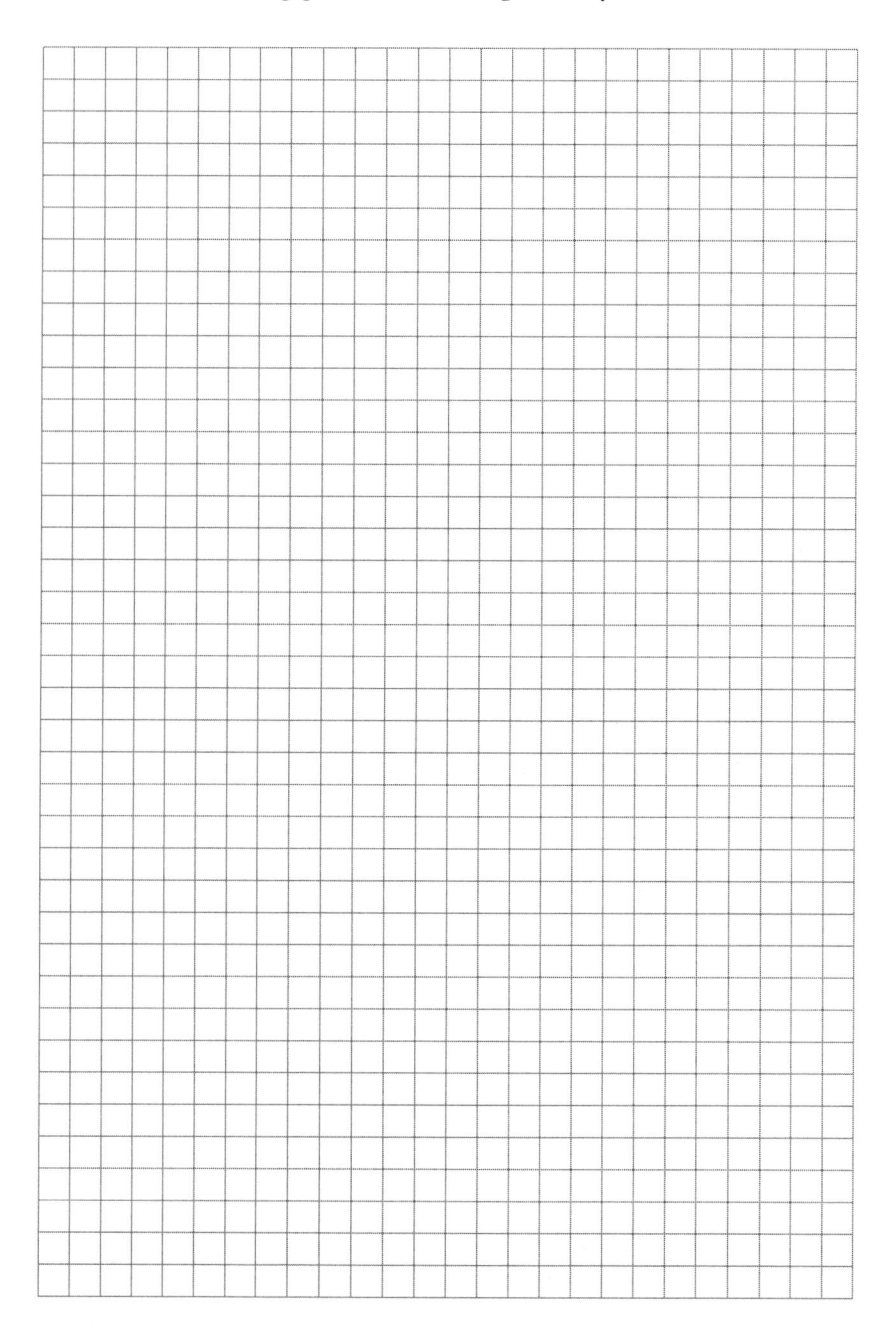

Does your house make you happy?

Now, do a walk through of your *dream* house. This is the best you that you can be. This is how you want all the aspects of your life to be. (Your house may not require all of these spaces; some spaces may fulfill more than one need.) Note the explanations that accompany each physical space.

Walk-Through List for Your <u>Dream</u> House

Location	Think About
« *Windows*	**Perspective.** They represent your clarity of vision. Are they stuck open or closed or draped. (Are our glasses half full or half empty? Is life "hard" or "easy?")
	Description: _____
« *Porch/ front yard*	**Approach.** What do visitors see and feel as they draw near? Is it approachable or not?
	Description: _____
« *Foyer*	**Boundary.** This is the point that separates entrants from going any farther, creating boundaries. Is it protective or secretive?
	Description: _____

« *Kitchen* **Nutritional center.** Is this place of service well nourished, malnourished, or indulged? Toxic? Is it food-less? Not just food but all types of nourishment.

DESCRIPTION: _____

_____

« *Dining room* **Sharing and companionship.** Is the room empty or filled with people, or do you eat in front of the TV?

DESCRIPTION: _____

_____

« *Bedrooms* **Rest and intimate relationships.** This is a place for rest, recuperation, and lovemaking/intimate relationships. Is it designed for two? Maybe two and a herd of animals? Is it more of an entertainment center?

DESCRIPTION: _____

_____

« *Living room* **Formal relations area.** This is for public relations including business relationships. Perhaps you're not a formal kind of person and all your relationships are informal?

DESCRIPTION: _____

_____

« *Laundry room* **Cleaning area.** Is it clean itself? Well stocked? Well lighted? Packed with stuff waiting to be put away? Do you clear/clean all unneeded/unused aspects of your life?

DESCRIPTION: _____

_____

« *Family room* **Recreation.** Is it for interaction or spectating? What do you do for fun?

DESCRIPTION: _____

_____

« *Study/library* **Introspective Space.** For learning, meditating, reflection. What thoughts fill your heart and mind when you are alone?

DESCRIPTION: _____

_____

« *Bathroom* **Remove toxins.** Wash away residue from the day; start a new day clean and fresh.

DESCRIPTION: _____

_____

« *Storage/closets/* **Storage/holding area/skeletons.** Are they full of junk,
basement unused stuff, things that no longer fit, things you're hiding?

DESCRIPTION: _____

_____

« *Doors* **Entrances and Exits.** Open/shut, locked, broken? How do we walk in and out of the world around us?

Description: _____

_____

« *Garage* **Adjuncts and storage.** Material things with a standard place in our world—not necessarily by choice (family obligations, etc.). How many cars? Clean or cluttered? Convenient? Detached? Automatic opener? Drive through?

Description: _____

_____

« *Décor/ artifacts* **Sentimental items.** Which pieces stand out and what room(s) are they in? What significance do they have for you? (Relate that to the room). Do they represent accomplishments and awards or scars and handicaps?

Description: _____

_____

« *Bonus room or anything omitted*

Description: _____

_____

CHAPTER SIX

Draw a blueprint of your <u>dream</u> house. Consider that this house is a reflection of the life you want to create:

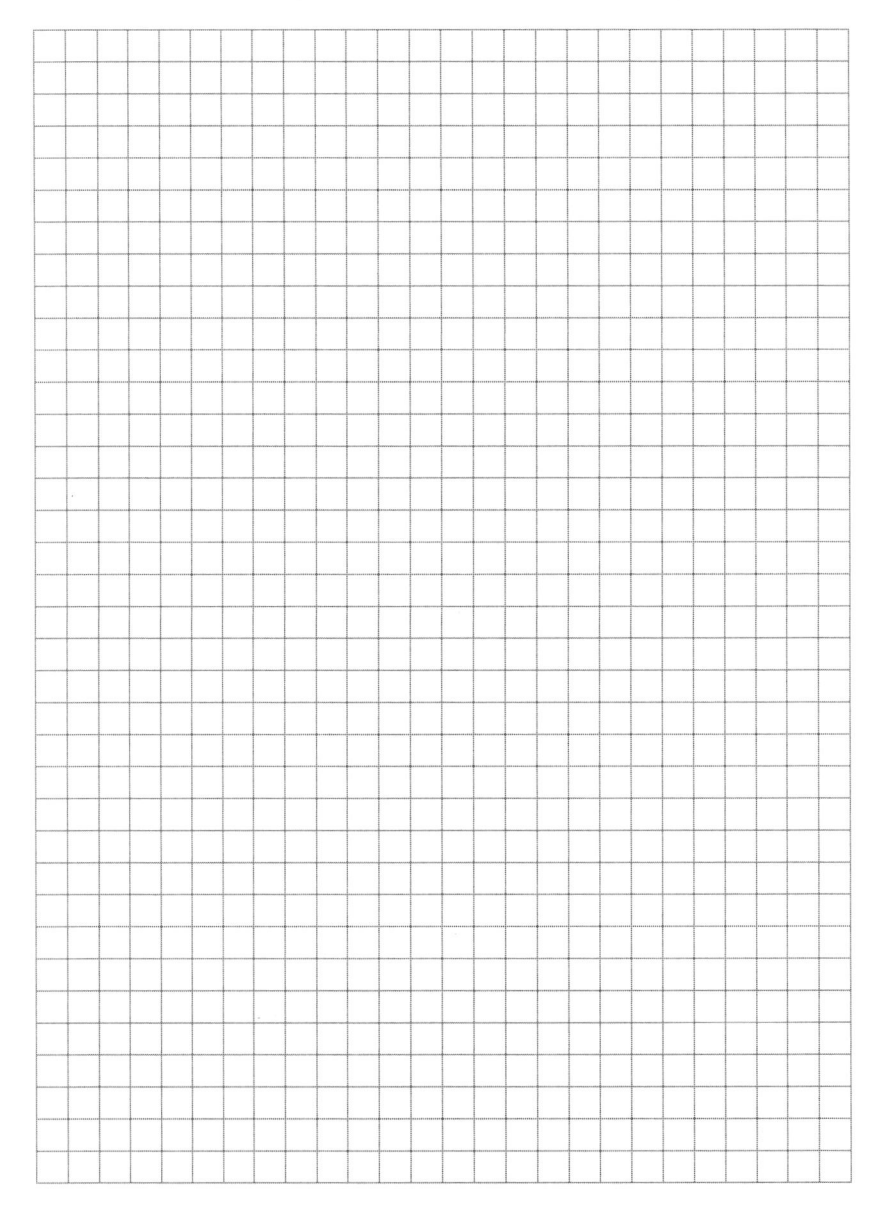

Would this new house make you happy? Is it consistent with the priorities you determined in the exercise in Chapter 5? Are you giving your priorities enough space?

Now compare your dream house to your current house. The differences are the changes that would have the most impact in your life. (For example: changing the size of your kitchen and making it more health oriented may indicate better nutrition, weight management, and health consciousness being actively addressed. These would satisfy a need for nurturing that is currently not being met.)

Consider changes you'd make between your current house and dream house and why. List these below:

Change	Why?
Example:	
« Foyer	Need to consider boundaries, privacy, and choosing who I want in my life and to what degree.
1) _____	_____
2) _____	_____
3) _____	_____
4) _____	_____
5) _____	_____

6) _____ | _____

7) _____ | _____

8) _____ | _____

9) _____ | _____

10) _____ | _____

Now that you have determined the differences, it is time to weigh your options:

- *Remodel.* Basically, things are fine; you just need some minor changes.
- *Renovate.* Major changes need to be made, but the basic structure can be salvaged.
- *Bulldoze and rebuild.* The basic structure cannot be changed or repaired. Your only choice is to start over.

As with any project, remember that you may get halfway into it and need to change your plan. You may be renovating and decide you only need to remodel. You may begin remodeling and determine that you must bulldoze and rebuild.

Be flexible and understand this will take longer than you think.

Remember that there will arise circumstances you will need to work around. (For example: You cannot divorce your mother). You will need to carefully consider whether or not compromises are worth the cost. Know that there is a solution for any problem that exists.

What changes do you need to make to build your dream house? Remodel or renovate or bulldoze and rebuild? Why?

_____

_____

_____

_____

_____

_____

_____

_____

_____

Now that you have completed your decision making and you have a blueprint for your new life, you will need a cost assessment. There are many costs when making serious changes in your life. You must review these costs, determine what you are willing to pay, and decide if you need to make changes to your plan (without sacrificing your happiness). Costs are usually thought of as the monetary aspect; however, costs of change can be emotional, physical, mental, and relationship related.

Assessing the Costs of Change

Type and Example of Costs	Costs
« **Emotional.** *Hurt feelings; someone close does not support my changes.*	_____ _____ _____
« **Mental.** *Anxiety over not getting the results I want within my time table.*	_____ _____ _____
« **Physical.** *Stress-induced aches and pains from lack of sleep.*	_____ _____ _____
« **Relationships.** *Letting go of relationships and people in my life that are unhealthy for me.*	_____ _____ _____
« **Financial.** *Cost of additional education, moving, etc.*	_____ _____ _____
« **Public life.** *Will my social standing or popularity be affected?*	_____ _____ _____

« **Other.** _____

_____

_____

Are you comfortable with these costs? Is your long-term happiness worth the price?

_____

_____

_____

_____

_____

_____

_____

You have now…

« Determined your priorities.
« Know the changes you want to make.
« Assessed the costs.

We are going to focus on *how* to accomplish the building of your soul's new home. We never said it was going to be easy. It will require work. Remember to enjoy the process. You are building the life you designed.

CHAPTER 7

• • •

Safety Training

BEFORE STARTING ANY construction project, you must undergo safety training. We want to make sure you stock your first-aid kit and know the safety rules. We have started your lists for you. Add the tools that work best for you.

First-Aid Kit

Here's a few ideas to get you started. Your kit is unique to you and the options you have chosen.
Contents may include:

1) Person outside of work and family for support.
2) Strengths list.
3) Weakness list (with how each weakness can be evolved into a strength).
4) Comfort aids such as favorite chocolate, safe sex, laughter, favorite movie/music…

5) _____

6) _____

7) _____

8) _____

9) _____

10) _____

The Safety Rules

1) **Pay attention to your physical well-being:**

   « Eat well.
   « Get adequate sleep.
   « Exercise.
   « Take nutritional supplements, as necessary.

   « _____

   « _____

   « _____

2) **Pay attention to your emotional well-being:**

   « Be mindful of your thoughts.
   « Express your feelings appropriately (don't hit people or blow things up).
   « Keep perspective.
   « Respect others.

   « _____

« _____

« _____

« _____

3) Manage stress:

  « Exercise.
  « Spend time with people who give you energy.
  « Spend time in places that give you energy and peace.
  « Meditate, pray.
  « Create some private space and use it often.

  « _____

  « _____

  « _____

  « _____

4) Pace yourself:

  « Avoid making too many changes at one time.
  « Prioritize your actions.
  « Think through your desires.
  « Plan how to execute the changes.
  « Move at a pace with which you are comfortable.

  « _____

  « _____

  « _____

5) **Avoid unhealthy trends,** which can obscure the road and make you stumble; these include:

   « Not sleeping, not eating/unhealthy eating, etc.
   « Excess use of alcohol.
   « Drugs.

   « _____

   « _____

   « _____

6) **Avoid poisons and toxins.** *This includes people. (Changes that you will be making will affect others, so address issues that arise with love and compassion.) Remember: Do no harm!*

   « _____

   « _____

   « _____

   « _____

   « _____

   « _____

7) **Clearing the view.** *Make sure your perspective is honest. The last thing you want to do is make a decision in haste that is based on a spur of the moment whim, a bad mood, or an insecurity. Consider whether the change you're contemplating is something you are unhappy with all the time or only occasionally. Ask yourself if you have patterns of self-sabotage. Have you ever really been happy? If not, will you know it when you are?*

- « If you say, "I'll be happy when…", why isn't it now? What will be different then? (Example: "When my kids are grown, I won't have all these responsibilities." Do you really think that when those responsibilities go away new ones won't replace them?)
- « If you say, "I'll be happy if…", why are you putting conditions on your happiness? (Example: "I'll be happy if my husband quits smoking." What if he quits smoking and starts chewing tobacco?)
- « If you say, "Life is hard…", what—other than eating, breathing, sleeping, and laughing—is life? And are those things really that difficult?
- « Are you really just making excuses for *not* being happy?

8) **Seek help when needed!** *Help is available for you twenty-four hours a day to assist you with things you cannot handle yourself. This help is comprised of your resource/solutions team. You are not alone!*

- « Personal coach.
- « Professional counselor.
- « Attorney.
- « Financial advisor.
- « Doctor.
- « Law enforcement.

- « _____
- « _____
- « _____
- « _____

Now, let's get started!

Hard Hat Zone

Chapter 8

• • •

Clearing the Clutter

GO THROUGH YOUR current house, room by room. Take an inventory of your life—real, physical stuff as well as your relationships. Remember, you have already "flushed" all the excuses.

What do you see everyday in your home that you hate to look at?

What do you look at everyday in your home, but don't *see*? Why is it still there?

What is trash?

Trash is defined as things, activities/duties, and people that:

« Can't be fixed.
« You don't like.
« Don't fit.
« Get in the way.
« Contribute nothing.
« Collect and attract dust and other contaminants.
« Are toxic.

We're not being mean here. These items are simply not what you want or need in your life now. One person's trash is another's treasure.

> **CAUTION** — Beware of dumping fees—but don't let the cost stop you from doing what you need to do.

What is treasure?

Treasure is defined as things, activities/duties, and people that:

- Make you happy.
- Add to the quality of your life.
- Bring out the best in you.
- Inspire you and give you energy.
- Bring you unconditional love.
- Collect and attract positive energy.

What are storage items?

Storage items are defined as things, activities/duties, and people that are not treasures…but you have no choice about them being in your life. Make sure that things and people classified in storage truly are things and people who must remain. Storage space is limited and costs you time, money, and energy—and takes up space you could fill with things and people that bring value to your life.

Determine whether these are in storage for the long-term or the short-term. Remember, too, that you will continually need to clean out the closets, attic, and basement. Therefore, you'll be dealing with these and incurring costs over and over again. Be careful what you store.

Trash (stuff to get rid of)

_____

_____

_____

_____

Treasures (stuff to keep)

Storage Items

Chapter 9

• • •

Finalize the Design: Taking Inventory and Stocking Your Toolbox

LET'S REVIEW HOW you've progressed. So far you have:

1) Designed your house (Chapter 6).
2) Decided whether to remodel or renovate or bulldoze and rebuild (Chapter 6).
3) Completed safety training (Chapter 7).
4) Decided what you currently have that you want to throw in the trash, keep as a treasure, or need to put away in storage for now (Chapter 8).

It's time to finalize your blueprint and stock your toolbox so that you can begin your project.

CHAPTER NINE

Finalize Your Blueprint

Review your dream house from Chapter 6 and make revisions as necessary to:

- « Make sure all the treasures you identified are included.
- « Provide space for the items that require storage.
- « Re-evaluate whether or not this defines happiness to you.
- « Review the blueprint against the expenses of the project to determine if you are willing to pay the cost.

Repeat this process until you are satisfied. **You are making a tremendous investment with your happiness at stake.** You don't want to finish and find yourself in a grass hut in the Rockies when you really wanted an igloo on a tropical island.

You made a list of changes in Chapter 6, and you've evaluated the costs and determined the trash, treasures, or items to be placed in storage. Now list the changes you've approved for the construction.

Changes You Want to Make

_____

_____

_____

_____

_____

_____

_____

Stock Your Toolbox

Be specific in completing this section. Your tools will be as unique as the details of your house. Start with your first-aid kit.

First-aid kit (from Chapter 7):

1) Choose a person outside of work and family for support—someone with your best interest at heart to keep you on the mark and help you monitor the costs.

   - « Choose this individual carefully. He/she must be confidential, supportive, and non-judgmental.
   - « Ensure that this individual will be able to be there for you.
   - « Share your project with this person, including the costs.
   - « Agree upon how and when you can communicate.

2) Carry the lists outlining your strengths and perceived weaknesses from Chapter 4. Keep these lists with you at all times. Restate those items here:

STRENGTHS:_____

_____

_____

_____

_____

_____

_____

Perceived Weaknesses: _____

_____
_____
_____
_____
_____
_____
_____

3) Add in your comfort aids, such as favorite chocolate, laughter, safe sex, favorite movie/music, etc. Determine what is healthy and appropriate for you, without hurting others (Chapter 7).

_____
_____
_____
_____
_____
_____
_____

Other possible tools to stock:

1) Temporary living space (Do you need "time out"? Safety? Space?).

_____

_____

_____

_____

_____

2) Financial stability (money in the bank, financing options).

_____

_____

_____

_____

_____

3) Physical preparation (Are there urgent health issues that need dealing with?).

_____

_____

_____

_____

4) Emotional preparation (Do you need to take a deep breath? Do you need to resolve fear issues?)

_____

_____

_____

_____

5) There are categories specific to your life that we could not anticipate. (Include those below).

Category:_____

_____

_____

_____

_____

Category:_____

_____

_____

_____

CATEGORY:_____

_____

_____

_____

_____

6) Chapter 2 (To remind you where you will be if you continue your current life).

7) Picture of your completed house for inspiration from Chapter 6. (Don't forget to color it.)

CHAPTER 10

• • •

Developing Your Construction Schedule

IN ORDER TO MAKE progress, you must develop a construction schedule. This schedule keeps you focused, moving forward, and reduces costly mistakes. We'll help you with your first item.

Construction Schedule

Identifying issues, goals, strategies, and completion dates.
(This section can be as long and as specific as you need.)

On the following pages, you will see four columns entitled "Issue to Deal with," "Goal," "Strategy," and "Completion Date." These are spread across both pages to give you room. The first column deals with *taking out the trash* (list in detail). The second is concerned with *ridding yourself of things and relationships that aren't working*. The strategy column *varies depending on the item being trashed*. The last column is self-explanatory.

We have started you out on the following page by giving an example and carrying it forward to demonstrate the process.

Issue to Deal with	Goal
Example:	
« *Abusive dead-end relationship*	*Get rid of drunk boyfriend*
1) _____	_____
2) _____	_____
3) _____	_____
4) _____	_____
5) _____	_____
6) _____	_____
7) _____	_____
8) _____	_____

Strategy	Completion Date
Move out or change locks while he's at work	*Before my birthday*

Issue to Deal with	Goal
9) _____	_____
10) _____	_____
11) _____	_____
12) _____	_____
13) _____	_____
14) _____	_____
15) _____	_____
16) _____	_____
17) _____	_____

Strategy	Completion Date

If you find yourself not taking action, review Chapter 2 that deals with your current reality projected into the future. Remember, **if you keep doing what you've always done, you'll keep getting what you've always gotten!**

Completion

Chapter 11

• • •

Celebrate!

EACH ISSUE RESOLVED on your construction schedule is a reason to celebrate. Since your life is always under construction, it is important to be happy during the process and to celebrate your accomplishments and each obstacle that you have overcome along the way.

Throw yourself a dream party:

- « Who did you invite?
- « How does it make you feel?
- « Are you celebrating each and every success?

On the following page, you should **start making celebration plans. You must be prepared when you complete each item on your construction schedule from the previous chapter.**

Celebration Plans

Example:

| « Ended toxic relationship | *Buy myself a nice piece of jewelry* |

1) _____ | _____

   _____ | _____

2) _____ | _____

   _____ | _____

3) _____ | _____

   _____ | _____

4) _____ | _____

   _____ | _____

5) _____ | _____

   _____ | _____

Congratulations! The hardest part is making the decisions and committing to the changes. The hardest part is over. Your construction schedule is complete.

It's time to celebrate!

Epilogue: Life Is an Ever-Changing Journey

As we've discussed, happiness is not a static condition. Events beyond your control, undesirable people making cameo appearances in your life, and personal growth and wisdom all change your perception or values. All of these things can cause fluctuations in your emotional state. That's normal. It's like a personal radio station that only plays your favorite songs. Every now and then, you lose the signal or the DJ tries to sneak some unknown artist onto the playlist. But these hiccups make you appreciate your personal list of classics even more or may even add to your list of current favorites.

Even more important: Just because you build your dream house doesn't mean you don't have to maintain it or clean it out every now and then. Major life changes can make you decide you need something bigger or you need to downsize. People may leave your circle and you feel compelled to replace them—or not. Jobs change and with them socio-economic status, which is sometimes crushing to our pride. Sometimes, though, the change is liberating.

Remember: The one thing that is a constant throughout your life is who you are based on the choices you've made. All of these changes are what they are: changes and circumstances, not *you* personally. How you *choose* to frame these events and move through them and how you *allow them* to influence you to be the kind of person you become is what the pursuit of happiness is all about.

Happiness doesn't drop into your lap. It's a deliberate effort on your part to focus your energy and efforts on what you value. It is setting healthy boundaries for those things that would pull you off the road. Your journey will be filled with bumps and curves and sometimes dead ends. This is part of being human. But your ability to get past them, smiling inside and out, is where happiness lives.

>With much joy and best
>wishes for a good journey,
>—*the authors*

Bookshelf

THERE ARE MANY good books on bettering your life. Here's a list of some of our favorites:

Albom, Mitch. *Tuesdays with Morrie*. New York: Doubleday, 1997.
Andrews, Ted. *Animal Speak*. St. Paul, MN: Hewellyn Pub., 2001.
A Blue Mountain Arts Collection: The Language of Happiness. Edited by Susan Polis Schultz. Boulder, CO: Blue Mountain Press, 1999.
Canfield, Jack and Mark Victor Hanson. *The Aladdin Factor*. New York: Berkley Publishing Group, 1995.
Canfield, Jack and Mark Victor Hansen. *Chicken Soup For the Soul*. Deerfield Beach, FL: Health Communications, Inc., 1993.
Carter-Scott, Ph.D., Cherie. *If Life is a Game, These are the Rules*. New York: Broadway Books, 1998.
Covey, Steven R. *Living the Seven Habits, Stories of Courage and Inspiration*, New York: Simon Schuster, 1999.
Das, Suraya. *Letting Go of the Person You Used to Be*. New York: Broadway Books, 2003.
Dr. Seuss. *On Beyond Zebra*. New York: Random House, Inc., 1955.
Dr. Seuss. *Oh, The Places You'll Go!* New York: Random House, Inc., 1990.
Dr. Seuss. *Oh, The Thinks You Can Think!* New York: Random House, Inc., Beginner Books, 1975.
Hay, Louise L. *You Can Heal Your Life*. Carlsbad, CA: Hay House Inc., 1999.
Hifler, Joyce Sequichie. *A Cherokee Feast of Days*. Tulsa, OK: Council Oak Books, 1992.
Kabat-Zinn, John. *Wherever You Go There You Are*. New York: Hyperion, 1994.

Lee, Robert J. and Sara N. King. *Discovering The Leader In You*. San Franciso: Jossey-Bass, 2001.

Ludin, Stephen C., John Christensen, and Harry Paul. *Fish!* New York: Hyperion, 2000.

McCullough, Mamie. *I Can. You Can Too!* Nashville: Thomas Nelson Publishers, 1987.

McCullough, Mamie. *Get It Together and Remember Where You Put It*. Dallas: Word Publishing, 1990.

McFarlane, Evelyn and James Saywell. *If…(Questions for the Game of Life)*. New York: Random House, Inc., Villard Books, 1995.

McNeely, Herman. *A Layman Looks at Prayer*. Lexington, NC: Herman L. McNeely Publication, 1966.

McWilliams, John-Roger and Peter McWilliams. *Life 101—Everything We Wish We Had Learned About Life In School, But Didn't*. Los Angeles: Prelude Press, 1991.

McWilliams, Peter. *Do It! Let's Get Off Our Buts*. Los Angeles: Prelude Press, 1991, 1994.

Mendelsohn, Jane. *I Was Amelia Earhart*. New York: Random House, Inc., Vintage Contemporaries, 1996.

Noer, David M.. *Breaking Free: A Prescription for Personal and Organizational Change*. San Francisco: Jossey-Bass, 2001.

Park, Elaine. *Join The Golden Rule Revolution*. Zelienople, PA: Caring Media, 2000.

Ray, Veronica. *Choosing Happiness—The Art of Living Unconditionally*. Center City, MN: Hazeldon Foundation, 1991.

Ruiz, Don Miguel. *The Four Agreements*. San Rafael, CA: Amber-Allen Publishing, Inc., 1997.

Rushnell, Squire. *When God Winks*. Hillsboro, OR: Beyond Word Publishing Inc., 2001.

Ryan, M.J. *The Power of Patience*. New York: Broadway Books, 2003.

Stock, Ph.D., Gregory. *The Book of Questions*. New York: Workman Publishing Company, Inc., 1987.

Vienne, Veronique. *The Art of Imperfection—Simple Ways to Make Peace With Yourself*. New York: Clarkson/Potter Publishers, 1999.

Acknowledgements

OUR EDITORS ALLOTTED us three pages to thank everyone who helped us on the journey to putting these thoughts on paper—we thank them for their generosity. But, we soon realized that if we actually tried to list everyone involved, we would inadvertently leave someone out and feel horrible about it. So let us say thanks to our friends, family, and loved ones who have supported us through this endeavor. Thank you to our editors at Whitline Ink for not screaming at the last minute changes (and for "getting" it). Thank you to the photography staff at Superieur Photographics, for capturing our sentiments on film. Thank you to the Grandover Resort, especially the waiters who were so diligent in keeping our coffee cups full and not fussing at us for occupying a table for hours at a time as we worked. And most of all, thank you to the people who were a pain in the neck, and the universe for all of the challenges and stumbling blocks it threw at us—you were the ones that taught us where to find the happiness inside.

—*C.J., Katrina, and Randall*

Authors

• • •

RANDALL HENION, PhD, is a retired public school superintendent. Currently he makes a living as professor, presenter, and coach in the areas of education, leadership, and personal development. He and his wife, Carolyn, live in a beautiful country home in Lexington, N.C.

KATRINA REDMON, CPA, is the former CFO of a construction company. She is a business consultant who also coaches and mentors others on focusing their lives and finding their dreams. When she's not globetrotting, she makes her home in Winston-Salem, N.C.

C.J. JOSEPH, MS, has owned and operated a training and coaching firm specializing in personal and professional development of "soft skills" for the past 10 years. When she's not up to her ears in volunteer work supporting a variety of community organizations or traveling she makes her home in Winston-Salem, N.C.

The three met by accident, became friends and co-authors by divine providence, and continue to work together to bring joy to as many people as they possibly can through books and seminars.

Authors' Note

● ● ●

IF YOU'D LIKE MORE information about individual seminars or would like to arrange a presentation of the guidelines within this book to your organization, group, or office, contact the authors via:

HJR Incorporated
PO Box 30236
Winston-Salem, N.C. 27130-0236
www.hjrinc.com

BOOK ORDER AND REQUEST FORM

Title	No. of Copies	Price Each	Total
The Road to Happy	_____	$11.95	$_____

S/H per book $3.00 $_____
subtotal $_____
7% N.C. sales tax $_____
total enclosed $_____

name ───────────────────────────

organization ───────────────────────

mailing address ─────────────────────

city ────────────────────────────

state ─────────────────── zip ──────────

phone ──────────── e-mail *(optional)* ────────

☐ YES! Please tell me how I can arrange to have the guidelines within this book presented to my organization.

Submit this completed form and make your check payable to:

HJR Incorporated
PO Box 30236
Winston-Salem, N.C. 27130-0236

The Road to HAPPY

cut here or simply photocopy page